Meteor

Perspectives on an asteroid strike

Alex Woolf

Raintree

Raintree is an imprint of Capstone Global Library Limited, a company incorporated in England and Wales having its registered office at 7 Pilgrim Street, London, EC4V 6LB – Registered company number: 6695582

www.raintreepublishers.co.uk
myorders@raintreepublishers.co.uk

Text © Capstone Global Library Limited 2015
First published in hardback in 2014
The moral rights of the proprietor have been asserted.

Edited by Andrew Farrow, James Benefield and Claire Throp
Designed by Philippa Jenkins
Original illustrations © Capstone Global Library Ltd 2014
Picture research by Tracy Cummins
Originated by Capstone Global Library Ltd
Printed in China

ISBN 978 1 406 28030 2
18 17 16 15 14
10 9 8 7 6 5 4 3 2 1

British Library Cataloguing in Publication Data
A full catalogue record for this book is available from the British Library.

Acknowledgements
We would like to thank the following for permission to reproduce photographs: AP Photo p. 10 (Nadezhda Luchinina, E1.ru); Corbis pp. 9 (© Mike Agliolo), 14 (© Andrei Ladygin/ZUMA Press), 16 (© Reuters/Andrei Kuzmin), 19 (© Reuters/Andrei Romanov), 20 (© Heino Kalis/Reuters), 35 (© Ikon Images), 36 (© Bettmann), 40 (© Marcelo Hernandez/dpa); Getty Images pp. 6 (Michael Dunning), 12 top (Andrey Rudakov/Bloomberg), 25 (Alison Wright/National Geographic), 27 (Mandel Ngan/AFP), 31 (The Asahi Shimbun), 32 (Yuri Kadobnov/AFP), 38 (Nicholas Kamm/AFP), 46 (Erik Simonsen), 49 (Keith Johnson); Landov p. 18 (EPA/Sergei Ilnitsky); Nasa pp. 43 (JSC/Orbital Debris Photo Gallery), 44 (National Aeronautics and Space Administration); Newscom pp. 22 (Andrei Ladygin/ZUMA Press), 26 (Oleg Kargopolov/AFP/Getty Images), 29 (Travis Heying); Science Source p. 34 (Valeriy Melnikov); Wikimedia p. 12 bottom (Anthony Ivanoff).

Cover photograph of a factory building in Chelyabinsk damaged by the shockwave of the meteorite fall on 16 February 2013, reproduced with permission of Newscom (Jiang Kehong/Xinhua/Photoshot).

Every effort has been made to contact copyright holders of material reproduced in this book. Any omissions will be rectified in subsequent printings if notice is given to the publisher.

Disclaimer
All the internet addresses (URLs) given in this book were valid at the time of going to press. However, due to the dynamic nature of the internet, some addresses may have changed, or sites may have changed or ceased to exist since publication. While the author and publisher regret any inconvenience this may cause readers, no responsibility for any such changes can be accepted by either the author or the publisher.

Contents

Some words are printed in bold, **like this**. You can find out what they mean by looking in the glossary.

DOSSIER:
THE CHELYABINSK METEOR

On 15 February 2013, a 10,000-tonne space rock, known as an asteroid, entered Earth's atmosphere over Russia. The asteroid was moving so fast that the air in front of it compressed (was squeezed). The friction of the air on the rock caused the rock to heat up and start to glow. Pretty soon it turned into a **meteor** – a dazzling fireball in the sky – which exploded some 23.3 kilometres (14.5 miles) above the province of Chelyabinsk in the southern Urals. The **shockwave** from this massive explosion was powerful enough to damage 7,200 buildings in six cities across the region, causing nearly 1,500 injuries. Fragments of **meteorite** fell to earth over a wide area. The Chelyabinsk meteor caused more damage, shock and injury than any meteor impact in recorded history.

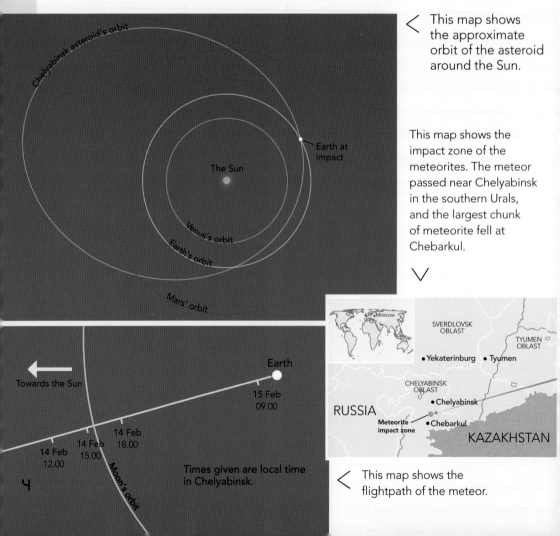

This map shows the approximate orbit of the asteroid around the Sun.

This map shows the impact zone of the meteorites. The meteor passed near Chelyabinsk in the southern Urals, and the largest chunk of meteorite fell at Chebarkul.

Chelyabinsk asteroid's orbit

Earth at impact

The Sun

Venus's orbit

Earth's orbit

Mars' orbit

Towards the Sun

Earth

15 Feb 09.00

14 Feb 18.00

14 Feb 15.00

14 Feb 12.00

Moon's orbit

Times given are local time in Chelyabinsk.

Moscow

SVERDLOVSK OBLAST

TYUMEN OBLAST

• Yekaterinburg   • Tyumen

CHELYABINSK OBLAST

• Chelyabinsk

RUSSIA

Meteorite impact zone

• Chebarkul

KAZAKHSTAN

This map shows the flightpath of the meteor.

ASTEROID TIMELINE

4.5 BILLION YEARS AGO
The asteroid forms during the early solar system

3.5 BILLION YEARS AGO
It collides with another asteroid, which causes it to fracture and drift closer to Jupiter. The gravitational pull of Jupiter sends the asteroid into a different orbit, moving it towards the inner solar system.

10 MILLION YEARS AGO
It collides once more with another celestial object, making it loose and spongy and causing it to disintegrate fairly easily when it enters Earth's atmosphere

FOR MILLIONS OF YEARS UNTIL MID FEB 2013
The asteroid slowly spirals closer to Earth, with many near misses, until it's caught by Earth's gravity and accelerates towards it

Our dangerous skies

So what exactly was this object that appeared in the skies over Russia on 15 February 2013, and where did it come from? The object, before it exploded, was an asteroid. These are small, airless, rocky worlds in orbit around the Sun. They range from boulders of 1 metre (3 feet) to minor planets of 950 kilometres (600 miles) in diameter, and they number in the millions.

Asteroid belt

Most of the asteroids we know about are in the asteroid belt, a region of the solar system lying between the orbits of Mars and Jupiter. Astronomers believe asteroids are the rubble left over from the formation of the solar system. The **gravitational influence** of Jupiter prevented any planets from forming in that region. Instead, the small objects that were there collided with each other, fragmenting into the asteroids we see today.

When asteroids and meteoroids strike Earth's atmosphere, they grow very hot and start to glow. These are visible in the night sky. We call them meteors or shooting stars.

Near-Earth asteroids

Not all asteroids are in the asteroid belt. Around 10,000 of them have an orbit that brings them close to Earth. These are known as near-Earth asteroids (NEAs) and they are the ones that may, possibly, collide with our planet. If 10,000 sounds like an alarmingly high number, don't worry too much: space is extremely big and the chances of an asteroid striking Earth are small.

Asteroids the size of the Chelyabinsk meteor hit us about once every 60 years. The reason we don't often hear about them is because most of Earth is made up of ocean and wilderness, and we simply don't notice the asteroids when they strike the planet. The other thing to remember is that Earth's atmosphere acts like a protective cushion, saving us from the worst effects of these impacts.

Monster asteroids

The atmosphere cannot protect us against really big asteroids, however. An asteroid with a 10-kilometre (6.25-mile) diameter, for example, could easily wipe out human civilization. But we'd be incredibly unfortunate to witness something like that, as they only strike about once every 100 million years. (You can read about the consequences of a really big asteroid strike in the fact panel below, and on pages 38–41.)

Chicxulub crater

We know for a fact that Earth has suffered many asteroid strikes in the past, because our planet still bears the scars of these impacts in the form of craters. One of the largest of these is the Chicxulub crater in Mexico. It is 180 km (111 mi.) wide, and the asteroid that formed it would have had a diameter of at least 10 km (6.2 mi.). By dating the rocks in the area, scientists have worked out that the asteroid struck around 65 million years ago. The force of the impact (equivalent to around 100 trillion tonnes of the explosive TNT) would have devastated Earth's climate for years, and many experts believe it caused the extinction of the dinosaurs.

Meteoroids

Although asteroids are relatively rare visitors, we get bombarded by smaller rocks, called **meteoroids** (under 1 metre/3.3 feet in diameter), all the time. In fact, around 15,000 tonnes of meteoroids enter Earth's atmosphere every year, and they can be any size from a grain of dust to a boulder. Meteoroids are the shattered fragments of asteroids, **comets**, the Moon or Mars, following a collision with another **celestial body**.

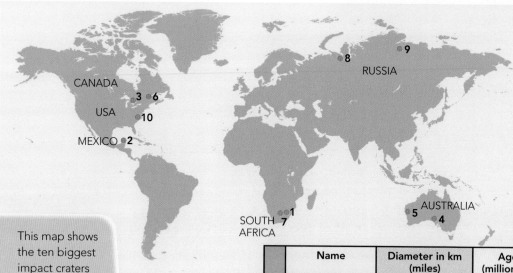

This map shows the ten biggest impact craters on Earth.

	Name	Diameter in km (miles)	Age (millions of years)
1	Vredefort	190 (118)	2,000
2	Chicxulub	170–300 (106–186)	65
3	Sudbury	130 (81)	1,800
4	Acraman	90 (56)	580
5	Woodleigh	40–120 (25–75)	364
6	Manicouagan	100 (63)	215
7	Morokweng	80 (50)	145
8	Kara	120 (75)	70.3
9	Popigai	100 (63)	35.7
10	Chesapeake Bay	85 (53)	35

Meteors

Most meteoroids never make it to Earth's surface. They enter Earth's atmosphere at tremendous speeds – up to 72 kilometres (45 miles) per second. When a body travelling at this speed passes through the atmosphere, it causes a great deal of friction. The meteoroid grows very hot and starts to glow. As it disintegrates, it forms a streak of light, which is visible in the night sky. We call these light trails shooting stars, or meteors. Meteoroids that survive this violent passage through the atmosphere and reach Earth's surface are known as meteorites.

Bolides and superbolides

Asteroids, such as the one that exploded over Chelyabinsk, are bigger than meteoroids, so they burn brighter. Because they are so bright, they often go by the name of **bolides**, or fireballs. The brightest are known as **superbolides**. The Chelyabinsk meteor was a "superbolide".

Comets

Asteroids are not the only space objects threatening us. There are also comets – balls of ice, dust and gas that orbit the Sun. When comets pass close to the Sun, their ice **sublimes** and they form spectacular dust-and-gas tails that can reach over 320 million kilometres (200 million miles) in length. A large comet could devastate Earth. However, such an event is even less likely than a large asteroid impact. Fewer than 100 near-Earth comets have been discovered. There is no proof that a comet has ever hit Earth, though some people think that a small one struck in 1908 (see pages 36–37).

The case of Ann Hodges

One of the first known cases of a meteorite injuring a human occurred on 30 November 1954 in Sylacauga, Alabama, USA. Ann Hodges, a 31-year-old woman, was taking a nap on the couch in her living room when a grapefruit-sized meteorite crashed through the roof, bounced off the radio and struck her on the side. She was badly bruised.

Big asteroid impacts are extremely rare. When they happen, the results are devastating for life on our planet.

The Chelyabinsk meteor

The morning of Friday 15 February 2013 began like any other in the city of Chelyabinsk in Russia. The sun rose at 9 a.m., its light gleaming on the peaks of the nearby Ural Mountains. People dressed warmly against the winter chill as they made their way to school or work. No one in the city could possibly know that a giant rock weighing more than the Eiffel Tower was speeding through the sky towards them at 50 times the speed of sound.

Fireball in the sky

At 9.20, people in Chelyabinsk noticed a burning fireball streaking across the sky to the south, heading from east to west. It was bright enough to cast moving shadows on the city streets. "I saw a flash in the window," said Maria Polyakova, head of reception at the Park-City Hotel. "I turned toward it and saw a burning cloud, which was surrounded by smoke and was going downward – it reminded me of what you see after an explosion." Valentina Nikolayeva, a teacher, described it as "an unreal light" that filled all the classrooms on one side of the school. "It was a light which never happens in life; it happens probably only in the end of the world."

A few people captured images of the fireball as it passed over the city of Chelyabinsk.

Air burst

The asteroid's enormous speed, combined with the shallow angle of its entry, generated so much heat and friction that it began to disintegrate. About 40 kilometres (25 miles) south of Chelyabinsk, at a height of 23.3 kilometres (14.5 miles), the meteor exploded. Around a fifth of the explosion's energy was released in the form of a bright flash of light lasting several seconds. Denis Kuznetsov, a historian, said that it shone "like 10 suns". The main explosion was followed by several smaller ones as the meteor continued to fragment.

Shockwave

The explosion occurred high enough above Earth to ensure that much of its energy was absorbed by the atmosphere. Nevertheless, when the shockwave hit Chelyabinsk and other nearby cities, it was still powerful enough to shatter windows and damage thousands of buildings. "My window smashed, I am all shaking! Everybody says that a plane crashed," tweeted local resident Katya Grechannikova.

The 1972 Great Daylight Fireball

On 10 August 1972, a fireball bright enough to be visible in daylight appeared in the skies above the western United States and Canada. The meteor didn't plunge to Earth, but grazed its atmosphere, making its closest approach at 58 kilometres (35 miles) over Montana, USA. The fireball sped northwards at 14.2 km (8.8 mi.) per second, leaving the atmosphere over Alberta, Canada. During its 100-second fly-by, the meteor was witnessed and photographed by many.

TIMELINE: CHELYABINSK ASTEROID

09.20.20
The asteroid enters the Earth's atmosphere over the Kazakhstan/Russia border.

09.20.33
The asteroid (now a superbolide meteor) reaches its peak brightness. This is also the approximate time of the explosion.

09.22.40
The explosion's shockwave reaches Chelyabinsk.

Chelyabinsk is a large city in Russia, approximately 1,500 kilometres (950 miles) east of Moscow. Built on the Miass River to the east of the Ural Mountains, the city is the centre of government of its local **oblast**, or province, also called Chelyabinsk. The city's name comes from *Chelyaby*, the name of an ancient village that had formerly stood on the site. In 1736, a Russian colonel founded a fortress there called Chelyaba, to protect surrounding trade routes from bandits. By 1787, the fortress had become the town of Chelyabinsk. The building of the Trans-Siberian Railway in the 1890s helped turn Chelyabinsk into an important centre of trade. During the era of the Soviet Union (USSR), Chelyabinsk experienced rapid industrial growth as a manufacturer of steel, tractors, tanks and other weapons. It remains a major industrial centre to this day.

Molten metal is poured into a cauldron aboard a railway wagon at Chelyabinsk's metallurgical plant. The city is one of Russia's main centres of heavy industry.

Kirova Street is a pedestrian street in central Chelyabinsk. As well as being an important industrial hub, Chelyabinsk is also a place of culture, with museums, theatres and educational establishments.

QUICK FACTS

POPULATION: 1.1 million

CLIMATE: January average temperature: -14.1°C (6.6°F); July average temperature: 19.3°C (66.7°F); annual rainfall: 430 mm (16.93 in.)

TRANSPORT: Bus, tram and trolleybus networks. A three-line underground network is due to open in 2017. The city is served by Chelyabinsk Airport.

TIME ZONE: YEKT (Yekaterinburg Time), six hours ahead of GMT (Greenwich Mean Time) and eleven hours ahead of **Eastern Standard Time (EST)**

CHELYABINSK CITY TIMELINE

1736
Fortress of Chelyaba is founded

1890s
Construction of the Trans-Siberian Railway turns Chelyabinsk into a major junction point and a gateway to the east

1897
Population reaches 20,000

1917
Population reaches 70,000

1930s
Chelyabinsk experiences rapid industrialization. The Chelyabinsk Tractor Plant and Metallurgical Plant are built.

1941
The Soviet leader Stalin moves military production east to avoid advancing German armies during World War II. This brings new factories and thousands of workers to Chelyabinsk. The city becomes known as Tankograd (Tank City). Chelyabinsk was virtually built from scratch during this time. Signs of the original town can be found in the city centre.

Shock and confusion

The first reaction to the fireball, the chain of explosions and the blast wave was shock. One witness said it seemed like an earthquake and thunder had struck at the same time. Another said the air smelled of gunpowder. "There was panic," said Sergey Hametov of Chelyabinsk. "People had no idea what was happening." Tyoma Chebalkin, a student, had a different impression: he reported that city-centre traffic was at a standstill and everyone was trying to place calls, but he saw no signs of panic.

Many children were in their lessons at the time the meteor struck. Classes stopped as pupils gathered at windows to watch the fireball streak across the morning sky. Was it a missile? A comet? A burning plane? They had to squint as the fireball suddenly blazed white – bright enough to cast shadows that slid swiftly across the ground. A series of explosions filled the air, followed by an eerie silence. Then, with astonishing force, the windows blew in.

The shockwave from the meteor strike smashed thousands of windows in Chelyabinsk.

Broken glass

Hundreds of video clips posted later online show ordinary mornings interrupted by a blinding flash and breaking windows. They show pupils and office workers thrown backwards across rooms as the air is filled with shattered glass. The shockwave was powerful enough to smash not only windows, but dishes, television screens and computer monitors in hundreds of homes and offices.

Communications down

In the immediate aftermath of the meteor strike, the city lost its internet and mobile phone access. This might have been because of damage to cables or phone masts inflicted by the shockwave, or the system might have crashed because everyone was logging on or making calls at once. For whatever reason, no one could communicate, increasing the general sense of alarm.

Rumours

Without any news, people developed their own theories of what had just happened. Chelyabinsk resident Valya Kazakov said some elderly women in his neighbourhood started crying out that the world was ending. Michael Garnett, Canadian-born goalkeeper for Traktor Chelyabinsk ice-hockey team, had some more down-to-earth theories. He thought it might have been "a natural gas leak or … a bomb or a missile or a plane crash". Alexander Yakovets, another local resident, reckoned it was a terrorist attack or military exercise. After an hour or so, the city's internet coverage was restored, and news that it had been a meteor strike began filtering through the stunned population.

Bright flash and broken windows

At around 8 p.m. on 26 November 1919, a meteor was sighted travelling east above southern Michigan and northern Indiana, USA. Witnesses said it resembled a brilliant illumination or a prolonged flash of lightning. In Athens, Michigan, the meteor was accompanied by thunder and heavy rain. The shockwave generated by the meteor's explosion broke windows and knocked out telephone communications and electrical supplies in several cities.

Injuries

Thousands of people gathered at windows to witness the event, not realizing they were in danger. The difference between the speed of light and sound meant that tens of seconds passed between the appearance of the flash and the **sonic boom** that blew the windows in (just as there is a delay between distant lightning and the sound of thunder). Russian television showed film of athletes at a city sports arena covered in blood after being showered by shards of glass from the arena's huge windows. Another video showed a long spear of glass slamming into the floor close to a factory worker.

No deaths were reported, but a total of 1,613 people asked for medical treatment, including 289 children. Sixty-nine of these stayed in hospital, including 13 children. Apart from cuts from broken glass, there were cases of **concussion** and broken bones. Some fingers and toes were reportedly amputated. One 52-year-old woman suffered a spinal fracture and had to be airlifted to Moscow for treatment. Others suffered from **post-traumatic stress disorder.** Most of the victims were from Chelyabinsk and surrounding villages; around 130 came from the nearby town of Kopeysk.

Many Chelyabinsk residents had to receive treatment after being injured by flying glass.

Damage

The shockwave from the meteor's explosion damaged some 7,200 buildings in six cities across Chelyabinsk Oblast. These included 3,724 flats, 671 educational institutions, 69 cultural facilities (museums, art galleries), 34 hospitals and clinics, 11 social centres and 5 sports venues. The walls and roof of a zinc factory partially collapsed. However, most of the damage was to windows – around 200,000 square metres (2.15 million square feet) of glass was reportedly shattered. Many of the buildings were also left without gas because of damage to the energy supply **infrastructure**.

Official reactions

Within hours of the meteor strike, the regional government of Chelyabinsk Oblast announced that all schools and kindergartens were closing for the day and children were to be sent home. This was because of the broken windows, which would put children at risk from injury, as well as exposure to the cold weather. Offices in downtown Chelyabinsk were evacuated for similar reasons. In a message on the regional government's website, residents were urged to stay at home if at all possible. Theatre shows were cancelled, as was an ice-hockey match featuring local side Traktor Chelyabinsk, after their stadium was damaged by the meteor.

Flying glass

Yekaterina Melikhova, a secondary school pupil, said she was in her geography class when a bright light flashed outside.

"After the flash, nothing happened for about three minutes," she said. "Then we rushed outdoors ... The door was made of glass, a **shock wave** made it hit us."

Yekaterina sustained cuts to her nose and upper lip.

Chelyabinsk resident Marat Lobkovsky said:

"I went to see what that flash in the sky was about. And then the window glass shattered, bouncing back on me. My beard was cut open, but not deep. They patched me up. It's okay now."

Operation Fortress

Shortly after the meteor strike, the Chelyabinsk authorities announced that police had been placed on high alert and had launched Operation Fortress to protect "vital infrastructure". They didn't say what infrastructure or why it needed protecting. It might not have been clear at this early stage that they were dealing with a meteor – perhaps some officials suspected a terrorist attack. There are several nuclear power stations in the region, and one immediate concern was that these might have suffered damage, causing a **radiation** leak. But the authorities quickly confirmed that radiation levels in the region were normal.

The shockwave caused part of a wall, as well as 600 square metres (6,000 square feet) of roof, at Chelyabinsk's zinc factory to collapse. The incident caused a temporary rise in world zinc prices.

A local resident holds up a fragment of meteorite collected in a snow-covered field near Chelyabinsk.

Meteorites

When the meteor exploded, it showered Chelyabinsk and the surrounding region with fragments of meteorite. These fell over an area of 100 square kilometres (39 square miles) across Chelyabinsk Oblast. Aleksandra Gerasimova, a retired milkmaid living in a village south of Chelyabinsk, reported being hit by a small meteorite that tore her coat and embedded itself in the inner lining.

One of the largest fragments discovered weighed more than 1 kilogram (2.2 pounds) and was found near Lake Chebarkul, 70 kilometres (43 miles) southwest of Chelyabinsk city. An even larger fragment broke through the ice covering the lake, creating an 8-metre (26-foot) diameter hole. A witness, who caught its landing on camera, saw it crash through the ice, sending up a jet of water. The fragment has now been retrieved. It measures 1.5 metres and weighs 570 kilograms.

The first known meteorite injury

On 28 April 1927, at about 9 a.m., a five-year-old girl was playing in the garden of her house in the village of Aba, Japan, when she suddenly cried out. Her mother rushed over to her and found she had suffered head injuries in two places, and a small piece of stone had lodged in her collar. The stone, later confirmed as a meteorite, was hot to the touch. The girl was the first recorded human victim of a meteorite. Fortunately, she recovered after a few days.

DOSSIER:
ASTEROID 2012 DA14

Just 16 hours after the meteor struck Chelyabinsk, a larger asteroid narrowly missed Earth. It passed a mere 27,743 kilometres (17,239 miles) above the planet's surface, within the orbits of over 100 weather and **telecommunication satellites**, and was visible through binoculars by observers in Australia, Asia and eastern Europe. That's the closest approach of any known object of that size. Understandably, people wondered whether the two incidents were related. **NASA** scientists confirmed that they weren't, because the asteroids approached Earth from different directions, had different orbits around the Sun and different compositions. It was just a massive cosmic coincidence!

< A man in Valencia, Spain, uses a telescope to search for Asteroid 2012 DA14.

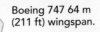

Boeing 747 64 m (211 ft) wingspan.

2012 DA14 asteroid approx 40 m (130 ft) max diameter.

Chelyabinsk meteor approx 17 m (56 ft) diameter.

Here we can see the sizes of 2012 DA14 and the Chelyabinsk asteroid, compared to some more familiar things. >

House 7.6 m (25 ft) height.

Person 1.8 m (6 ft) height.

DISCOVERED BY: the Observatorio Astronómico de La Sagra, Granada, Spain

ORBITAL PERIOD: 368 days, which shortened to 317 days after its encounter with Earth

SHAPE AND SIZE: elongated rock about 20 x 40 m (65 x 130 ft.)

SPEED: 7.8 km per second (17,400 mi. per hour)

RISK: asteroids of this size are expected to impact Earth about once every 1,500 years and would produce an **air burst** equivalent to 2.1 **megatons** of TNT, enough to devastate a town or city

ASTEROID 2012 DA14 TIMELINE

23 FEBRUARY 2012
The asteroid is discovered

9 JANUARY 2013
The asteroid is re-observed by Las Camapanas **Observatory**, Chile

15 FEBRUARY 2013
The date of its closest approach to Earth

15 FEBRUARY 2046
Expected date of its next close approach to Earth

16 FEBRUARY 2123
Expected date of its next close approach of similar distance to the 2013 encounter

The emergency services

We've looked at the experience of ordinary citizens caught up in the event, but how did the emergency services cope? The day after the meteor strike, an "emergency situation regime" was set up in the worst-affected towns and cities in Chelyabinsk Oblast: Chelyabinsk, Kopeysk, Yuzhnouralsk, Korkino and Yemanzhelinsk. Around 24,000 emergency workers were mobilized from across the region, in order to sweep up broken glass, board up holes and fit new windows. With temperatures falling below -20°C (-4°F), repairs had to be done quickly.

Dealing with the injured

Meanwhile, hospitals and medical staff handled the sudden influx of patients efficiently, thanks in part to the minor nature of most injuries. "The wounds that people have are mainly cuts and bruises, due to windows and window frames breaking and flying around," commented local surgeon Vladimir Basmannikov. Surgeon Sergey Vasilyev said that the blast broke a lot of windows in the hospital where he worked: "All surgeries were cancelled and we moved to the office where patients with broken glass

The clean-up process begins in Chelyabinsk following the meteor strike. Within days of the incident, many shops had reopened for business.

wounds started to arrive ... We have operated on 15 patients with multiple wounds of the face, head, hands and body. Fortunately, there were several surgeons from different cities coming for **plastic surgery** training to our department so we could work in three operating rooms simultaneously."

Return to normality

Most of those injured made quick recoveries. A month after the meteor strike, 65 of the original 69 admitted to hospital had returned home. Repairs to essential buildings were carried out quickly. By 19 February, the region's schools and hospitals had all reopened. Over the next few days, the Emergency Situations Ministry announced that more than 160 tonnes of broken glass had been removed and almost 10,000 windows mended in 5,700 buildings. Some Chelyabinsk residents were taking no chances: in case of another meteor strike, they reinforced their window panes with paper bands – a tip they learned from survivors of German air raids during World War II, more than 70 years earlier.

Contrasting reports

On 5 March, the region's vice-governor, Sergei Komyakov, announced that 98 per cent of the damage had been repaired and the emergency situation regime was over. The rest of the work will be completed "within five or ten days", he promised. However, according to a report by journalist Svend Buhl, by mid-April, less than 40 per cent of the damage had been repaired – many homes and public buildings still lacked windows, and the city's airport and ice rink continued to bear the scars of the shockwave. Yet, claimed Buhl, the government's emergency relief fund had already been spent.

A new era

Chelyabinsk governor Mikhail Yurevich described 15 February as the city's second birthday (the city's official birthday is 13 September, the date of its founding in 1736):

"If the meteor, which exploded above us, was just a little bigger, it's hard to imagine what could have happened to our towns and villages."

A mayor's perspective

Most people in a disaster zone will be concerned with saving themselves or their families. If they are doctors or rescue workers their responsibilities will extend to helping other individuals affected. However, there are some people who have to think about the whole community. One is the mayor of a city. Have you ever thought about the difficult decisions people have to make when there's a disaster? Imagine you are the mayor of a city of 2 million people. Your city has just been hit by the shockwave of an exploding meteor. As mayor, it's your job to coordinate a response to this disaster.

You receive the following reports:

- Internet and phone networks are down in many parts of the city, meaning that any announcements made on your website won't be heard by a large proportion of the population.
- At least 150 people have been killed and their bodies have been found lying in the streets or inside buildings.
- So far, around 3,000 people have called the national emergency phone line summoning ambulances, or gone to A&E departments of hospitals with injuries, mainly cuts from broken glass.
- Thousands more victims may still be stuck in their houses unable to get through to emergency services because of the communication breakdown.
- Thousands of buildings across the city, including schools, hospitals, shops, offices and blocks of flats have suffered damage.
- Hundreds have been made homeless and will need emergency shelter, food and medicine.
- There are at least five fires raging out of control in the city.
- There has been **looting** and violence in several high streets where shops have been abandoned by their owners.

Your resources are limited:

- You have 100 ambulances at your disposal – not enough to deal with all the wounded in the city who need taking to hospital.
- You have 40 fire engines – again, not enough to deal with all the fires.
- It will be 10 hours before more ambulances and fire engines are made available by other regional authorities.

- 2,000 emergency workers are immediately available for (a) search and rescue, (b) clean-up duties, (c) repairs to the communications networks.
- 8,000 police officers are immediately available for helping to (a) maintain public order, (b) coordinate a city-wide evacuation, (c) organize emergency shelter.
- A further 40,000 police and emergency workers can be brought in from other regional authorities over the next 24 hours.

It is up to you to make decisions about what actions to take and how to prioritize them.

Now that you've seen the disaster from the perspective of someone who has to make the decisions, do you think it is surprising that the authorities are so often criticized for their handling of disaster relief?

A major challenge facing emergency services after any natural disaster is dealing with refugees. Camps need to be established quickly, with adequate food, shelter, medical care and sanitation, if a second humanitarian disaster is to be avoided.

Public reaction

The meteor strike on Chelyabinsk was so sudden and unexpected that people's first reaction was, naturally, a mixture of panic and confusion. Gradually, however, as they learned the truth of what had happened, other perspectives and responses emerged, including humour, greed, excitement, pride and suspicion.

Media response

As is often the case with natural disasters and other fast-breaking news stories, **media** outlets initially struggled to keep up with events. Rather than offering detailed reports that would be out of date almost as soon as they were published, news websites put out short bulletins, continually updating the story with the latest information as it emerged. For example, the Russia Today (RT) network's website published live updates every few minutes, and photos and video footage of the fireball. A lot of early coverage of the event focused on the remarkable coincidence of a meteor arriving on the same day as asteroid 2012 DA14 (see pages 20–21).

Russia's Emergencies Minister, Vladimir Puchkov (in red), is accompanied by journalists and photographers as he inspects the damage to a sports centre in Chelyabinsk following the meteor strike.

This meteorite fragment, on display at the White House, Washington, DC, came from Mars. It was ejected by Mars by the impact of an asteroid, and then landed on Earth.

Cashing in

Money-making instincts did not take long to surface. When the government announced that it would offer financial compensation to those who suffered damage in the meteor strike, it was reported that many locals deliberately broke their windows. They were expecting that the money they would receive from the government would be more than it cost them to replace the windows.

Within hours, "fragments of meteorite" were being offered for sale. "Selling meteorite that fell on Chelyabinsk!" a dealer called Vladimir announced on a popular Russian auction website. Within days, there were offers of "Chelyabinsk meteorite fragments" ranging from £20 to £11,000, from sellers as far away as Portugal, Germany, Finland and Latvia. The meteorite rush soon faded as public suspicions grew that most, if not all, of these stones were fake.

Breaking the news

News of the mysterious fireball and explosion initially spread via social media and local radio. Bizarrely, the first non-Russian news outlet to spread word was an ice hockey blog called *Russian Machine Never Breaks* based in Washington, DC, USA. It published a report about the explosion (they didn't yet know the cause) at just after 11 p.m. Eastern Standard Time (EST), within an hour of the event and before the Russian government had made any announcement. The blog's editors had been keeping a close eye on ice-hockey team Traktor Chelyabinsk, and a tweet from their goalkeeper Michael Garnett had alerted them. An official Russian announcement that "at least one meteorite has fallen in Chelyabinsk region" was made about an hour after the event, and confirmed by Associated Press on Saturday 16th at 12.21 a.m. EST.

Meteor products

One enterprising food manufacturer applied to the Russian patent agency to register a new range of meteorite-related food products. And local businessman Sergei Andreyev announced plans to launch a new perfume named Chebarkul Meteorite, which will feature "metallic and stony notes [scents]".

Fireball footage

Fascination with the event went global over the weekend of 16–17 February, greatly helped by the dramatic footage of the fireball captured on "**dashcams**" – video cameras that Russians keep mounted on the dashboards of their cars. Within 15 hours of the event, dashcam videos of the meteor had been viewed millions of times on YouTube and other video-sharing websites.

Meteorite hunters

In the days following the event, something akin to a "gold rush" gripped the people of Chelyabinsk, as thousands began combing the snow-covered countryside for meteorite fragments. Among those searching were the Belizkaya family. The meteor explosion had scared them at first – it cracked their ceiling and filled their home with oven soot. But they soon came to see it as something positive. On finding a meteorite fragment, Elena Belizkaya said, "this is such a memento of that event. We'll keep it at home for now, but if there's a chance to sell it, we'll sell some, of course!"

Jilin City meteor

On 8 March 1976, a meteor exploded over the outskirts of Jilin City in northern China. There was a giant boom followed by a series of quieter bangs lasting 4 or 5 minutes and heard by over a million people. Around 4 tonnes of meteorite fragments rained down over an area greater than 800 sq. km. (309 sq. mi.). A survey team sent out by the Chinese Academy of Science collected hundreds of meteorites. They turned out to be **chondrites** – typical meteorites, made from an **accretion** of dust and grit from the early solar system. The heaviest, weighing 1,766 kg (3,894 lbs.), remains the largest chunk of chondrite ever found.

American meteorite hunter Steve Arnold pulls a homemade metal detector across a wheatfield near Haviland, Kansas. The device has helped Arnold discover a large meteorite buried in the ground.

Most meteorites were pea-sized but some were as large as golfballs. They made mouse-hole-like craters in the snow. "It's like hunting or fishing," said one meteorite hunter. "When you see an animal, your heart starts to beat fast… This is the same – you see a tiny hole, try it, and here it is."

Conspiracy theories

In the wake of the fireball and explosion over Chelyabinsk, a Moscow daily newspaper polled its readers on what they thought it was. Barely half believed the official "meteor" story. The rest preferred to believe in a variety of other explanations given by some of Russia's more colourful characters.

Russian politician Vladimir Zhirinovsky claimed that the United States must have staged a secret weapons test over Chelyabinsk. "Nothing will ever fall [from space]," he told journalists. "If something falls, it's people doing that. People are the instigators of wars…"

Was the meteor blown up?

A controversial yet influential Russian scientist, Yury Lavbin, claimed a UFO saved Chelyabinsk by destroying the meteor before it could land. His followers pointed to a dashcam video that, they claimed, shows this happening.

Another rumour was that local air defence units intercepted the meteor and blew it up to prevent it falling on the city. The regional Emergencies Ministry had to deny this story.

The phantom text message

In the hours following the event, a spokesperson for the Urals regional Emergencies Ministry claimed a mass SMS had been sent out, warning Chelyabinsk residents of the meteor. Locals denied ever receiving a message. The Emergencies Ministry later denied any message was sent and the spokesperson was sacked for spreading false information.

Environmental concerns

Some were more worried about the potential threat posed to the environment by the event. Vladimir Chuprov of Greenpeace Russia pointed out that the meteor struck just 96 kilometres (60 miles) south-east of the Mayak nuclear storage and disposal facility, which stores **weapons-grade plutonium** and **radioactive waste**. A similar distance to the north-east is the chemical weapons disposal facility at Shchuchye, which contains some 6,000 tonnes of **nerve agents**, including sarin and VX. If the explosion had occurred only a little further east, these facilities might have been damaged, causing leaks of highly toxic substances.

Taking pride in the superbolide

Chelyabinsk is already making plans to exploit its newfound fame. The regional government has said it wants to be known as the Meteorite Capital of Russia. Various proposals have been put forward. These include hosting an annual "cosmic music and fireworks festival", or building a meteorite museum, a "cosmic water park" or a Disney-style theme park that recreates the earth-shaking, window-shattering events of 15 February. Others would like to brighten up Chelyabinsk city by painting space landscapes on its drab offices and blocks of flats. The mayor of Chebarkul, Andrei Orlov, plans to build a diving centre at the lake so tourists can search for meteorites in its muddy bed.

Tours and exhibitions

Within weeks of the event, a Japanese tourist company was selling group tours to the city and the impact site, priced at £528 per person, and the city's history museum had installed a "Meteor Day" exhibit – a meteorite fragment surrounded by the front pages of newspapers from the day. The Museum of Local Lore planned an exhibition called The Space Wanderer: Eyewitness Accounts, in which visitors could view photos, dashcam stills and a film made shortly after the explosion.

"Space sent us a gift, and we need to make use of it. We need our own Eiffel Tower or Statue of Liberty."

Natalia Gritsay, head of the Chelyabinsk tourism department

"Nobody had heard about us and now all the world knows. We can earn some dividends [profit] on that. If there'll be a massive tourist inflow, we'll build more hotels."

Chelyabinsk Governor Mikhail Yurevich

This hole in the ice covering Chebarkul Lake marks the site where the largest fragment of meteorite struck. The lake is now a tourist destination.

Scientists at work

A huge meteor strike observed and recorded by so many eyewitnesses is rare, so scientists were excited by the opportunity to study it. Using the data, they were able to work out with surprising accuracy the nature of the superbolide, its mass, speed and **trajectory**, and the energy it released when it exploded. In fact, most of the facts on pages 4–5 were known within a day or so of the event.

Calculating its speed and mass

The Chelyabinsk fireball was the most widely recorded meteor strike in history. Scientists studied huge amounts of time- and date-stamped video footage from dashcams, camera phones and traffic cameras uploaded to the web. They were further helped by images of the shadows cast by street objects, marking the passage of the fireball.

The first video showed the asteroid at the moment it began to glow. The **gradient** of flight was about 20 degrees, and by calculating the angles from which the fireball was filmed, they could determine the height at which it broke up. It took about 10 seconds from entry to break-up, which told them its speed. Once they knew the speed, angle and atmospheric heating of the superbolide, they could establish its mass.

By studying video footage, scientists were able to calculate the exact speed, mass and trajectory of the meteor.

Origin of the meteor

Jorge Zuluaga and Ignacio Ferrin, astronomers from Colombia, used the video footage, as well as their knowledge of the impact site of the main fragment in Lake Chebarkul, to reconstruct the meteor's orbit around the Sun. It took an elliptical (oval-shaped) path beyond the orbit of Mars to well within Earth's orbit. They worked out that it was a near-Earth asteroid, probably originating from the asteroid belt.

Research by brothers Carlos and Raúl de la Fuente Marcos from the Complutense University of Madrid, Spain, suggests that the meteor may have been a fragment of a larger, 200-metre (650-feet) wide asteroid called 2011 EO. This asteroid regularly crosses Earth's orbit and is already listed as potentially hazardous. It is one of a cluster of around 20 asteroids, which are thought to be remains of an even bigger rock that broke up between 20,000 and 40,000 years ago.

Explosive energy

Peter Brown of London, Ontario, Canada, is a world expert at analysing fireballs using infrasound – that is, sound waves below the range of human hearing. Infrasound reveals the energy of a fireball's explosion: the lower the frequency, the bigger the blast.

Humans can't hear frequencies below 20 **Hertz**. The energy of the Chelyabinsk blast had a frequency of 0.03 Hertz, so low that Brown had to modify the software he was using. The shockwave was the most powerful ever recorded. In fact, a monitoring station in Greenland revealed that the sonic boom lapped Earth at least three times.

Infrasound monitoring stations

Peter Brown used readings taken from infrasound monitoring stations. There are 60 of these stations in 35 countries around the world. They detect nuclear explosions and ensure countries follow the worldwide ban on **nuclear tests**. They are also used to measure things like meteor explosions.

Fragile rock

Scientists studying video of the fireball's final airborne seconds could immediately see clues to its composition. Pavel Spurny from the "fireball studies" team based at Ondrejov Observatory, Czech Republic, observed that it was "relatively fragile in comparison with other superbolides". Due to its possible collision around 10 million years ago (see page 5), the asteroid was described as "fairly loose and spongy", causing it to disintegrate quite easily when it entered Earth's atmosphere. Erik Galimov, director of the Institute of Geochemistry at the Russian Academy of Sciences, said the asteroid probably received multiple cracks as a result of the collision, which caused the meteor's powerful explosion.

Studying the meteorites

Russian scientists and volunteers were soon scouring the area around Chebarkul where most of the meteorites fell, in order to collect samples for analysis. Larry Taylor, director of the Planetary Geosciences Institute at the University of Tennessee, USA, assumed the meteor must have been full of volatile material (substances that evaporate easily) to cause such an explosion. However, when the first meteorite samples were studied in the laboratory, it quickly became clear that it was a chondrite, a very common type of meteorite.

It was composed of about 90 per cent silicate, a stony substance made up of minerals such as olivine, pyroxene and troilite. The remainder consisted of metals, including zinc, iron, chrome and aluminium. Professor Viktor Grokhovsky of the Institute of Physics and Technology at Ural Federal University, who led the expedition to collect the meteorites, says chondrites are the same age as the solar system – about 4.5 billion years old.

A researcher at the Vernadsky Institute in Moscow, Russia, uses a microscope to analyse meteorite fragments found at Cherbarkul.

Asteroids frequently collide with each other in space. Those that survive such impacts are often weakened by them. The Chelyabinsk meteor may have been weakened by an earlier impact.

Iron meteorites

We should be thankful that it was a chondrite. According to Phil McCausland, an Earth Science professor at the University of Western Ontario, if the meteor had been the much rarer "iron" type (made of 95 per cent iron-nickel alloy), it would have impacted on the ground, rather than exploding in the atmosphere, due to its greater density and mass, causing far greater devastation. As it was, no more than 10 per cent of the meteor's weight (around 1,000 tonnes) hit Earth's surface, according to Erik Galimov. The impact released barely a kiloton of energy, compared to 440 kilotons released by the atmospheric explosion.

The Pribram meteorite

On 7 April 1959, a meteor struck east of Pribram in the Czech Republic. The fireball exploded 13 km (8 mi.) above Earth. It was the first meteor to be tracked by several cameras. By studying the video recordings, scientists determined the meteor's orbit and landing place. Four pieces of meteorite were found, the largest weighing 4.43 kg (9.76 lbs).

As scientists began to take account of the events of 15 February 2013, many were struck by their similarity to the Tunguska event, which took place over a hundred years earlier. In 1908, a massive explosion occurred near a remote river in Siberia, Russia, some 5,000 kilometres (3,106 miles) east of Chelyabinsk. Scientists believe the explosion was caused by an asteroid or comet entering Earth's atmosphere.

As with Chelyabinsk, theories soon began to circulate. Many Russians thought it was a sign that the end of the world was approaching; others believed it was caused by the crashing of an alien spacecraft. However, most experts believe that the Tunguska event was caused by the air burst of an asteroid or comet, 60–190 metres (200–623 feet) in diameter, 5–10 kilometres (3–6 miles) above Earth's surface.

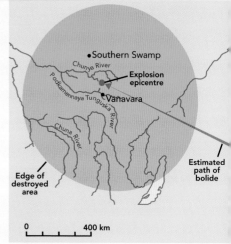

This diagram shows the location and approximate flightpath of the 1908 asteroid or comet.

> •Southern Swamp
> Chunya River
> Podkamennaya Tunguska River
> Explosion epicentre
> Vanavara
> Chuna River
> Edge of destroyed area
> Estimated path of bolide
> 0   400 km

Leonid Kulik led a series of expeditions to the site of the Tunguska event in the 1920s and 1930s. They took photographs to record the devastation.

EVENT: the Tunguska event

LOCATION: near the Podkamennaya Tunguska River (now Krasnoyarsk Krai), Siberia, Russia

DATE AND TIME: 30 June 1908 at approx. 07:14 local time (00:14 GMT).

PROBABLE CAUSE: air burst from an asteroid or comet entering Earth's atmosphere

ESTIMATES OF THE BLAST ENERGY: 10–15 megatons of TNT (approx. 1,000 times more powerful than the atomic bomb dropped on Hiroshima, Japan, in 1945), making it the largest impact event in recorded history

EFFECTS: flattened approximately 80 million trees over an area of 2,150 sq km (830 sq. mi.); broke windows hundreds of kilometres away; caused glowing sunsets in Asia and Europe over the following nights, probably due to dust particles thrown into the atmosphere

TUNGUSKA EVENT TIMELINE

1908
The Tunguska event happens

1921
Russian mineralogist Leonid Kulik visits the Podkamennaya Tunguska River basin and determines that the explosion was caused by a giant meteorite impact

1927–1937
Kulik leads several expeditions to the impact site and is shocked to find a vast area of trees scorched and stripped of branches – but no crater

1938
Kulik arranges an aerial survey of the area

1960s
The shape and extent of the zone of levelled forest is established. It resembles a vast butterfly shape 70 x 55 km (43 x 34 mi.).

2010
An expedition by scientists from the Troitsk Innovation and Nuclear Research Institute (TRINITY) uses **ground-penetrating radar** to examine the Tunguska site. They find fragments of the celestial body. Analysis shows it was a huge piece of ice that shattered on impact, supporting a theory that a comet caused the explosion.

What might happen?

We've seen what happens when an asteroid the size of a small building, like the one that hit Chelyabinsk, strikes Earth. The disaster was serious, but manageable. Now let's speculate on what might happen if a larger asteroid struck – say, one 1,000 metres (3,280 feet) wide. Let's say it enters the atmosphere at an angle of 45 degrees and is moving at 18 kilometres (11 miles) per second.

Impact

In this case, the atmosphere is no barrier. Unlike smaller asteroids and meteoroids, a large asteroid isn't slowed much by air friction, and it punches through the atmosphere as if it's hardly there. What *does* stop the asteroid is Earth itself. The collision creates a 60,000 megaton explosion. (The largest nuclear bomb ever built was less than 70 megatons, so it would be almost 1,000 times more powerful.)

With around 70 per cent of Earth covered by ocean, the asteroid probably strikes water, but wherever it lands, the impact **vaporizes** the asteroid and forms a crater (or cavity in the ocean) approximately 20 kilometres (12.5 miles) wide.

The tsunami that hit Japan in March 2011 was triggered by an undersea earthquake. Tsunamis caused by an asteroid striking the ocean could cause even greater devastation.

Tsunamis and earthquakes

A land impact generates massive earthquakes that devastate nearby human settlements. An ocean landing creates **tsunamis** – enormous waves up to several kilometres high – that radiate outwards in all directions from the impact zone. Travelling at around 300 kilometres (186 miles) per hour, these waves inflict massive destruction and flooding on every coastline.

The impact ejects thousands of tonnes of superhot matter into the air, including vaporized asteroid, material from Earth's crust, and – if it lands in the ocean – steam. It blasts this 100 kilometres (62.5 miles) into the sky, rising through a hole previously torn through the atmosphere by the asteroid as it fell (the asteroid is so big and fast, it pushes aside the air in front of it, creating a brief vacuum).

Impact winter

Some of this superhot ejected material falls back to Earth, starting mass fires around the globe. The rest spreads through the upper atmosphere, creating a blanket of dust around Earth thick enough to dim the sunlight. The fires send tonnes of smoke and soot into the air, making the sky even dimmer. The lack of sunlight reduces global temperatures and creates an "**impact winter**".

Scientists don't always agree on the after-effects of a giant asteroid strike:

"The vast amount of debris thrown up from the explosion and the subsequent fires will create an 'asteroid winter' that might persist for several years, long enough for crop failures to lead to mass starvation."

From the website of the Asteroid Terrestrial-impact Last Alert System (ATLAS) Project

"I feel that the threat of a dust-generated 'impact winter' is vastly overstated and that ... [it] will not be anywhere near as severe ... as some predict."

James A. Marusek writing for the American Institute of Aeronautics and Astronautics, 2007

Global warming and UV radiation

After a few months, the dust settles, the sunlight brightens, and the impact winter comes to an end. However, the disaster for Earth's inhabitants is far from over: there follows a prolonged period of global warming – the **carbon dioxide** put into the atmosphere by the mass fires creates a **greenhouse effect**. With an ocean impact, there could be a further problem: the seawater vapour ejected into the upper atmosphere contains chemicals that destroy the **ozone layer**, which protects us from the Sun's **ultraviolet (UV)** radiation.

The effect on life

What is the effect of this speculative asteroid strike on humans, animals and plant life? At first, there is chaos and panic in and around the impact zone. People living there experience earthquakes, tsunamis, floods and fires. Casualties run into millions as the asteroid falls near large cities and hits an ocean near a heavily populated coastline.

Shops were raided by looters following an earthquake in Concepción, Chile, in February 2010. An asteroid impact could cause a similar breakdown in law and order as people struggle to survive.

As the sky dims and the impact winter exerts its grip, the whole world starts to feel the effects of the asteroid strike. The reduction in sunlight slows down plant **photosynthesis**, threatening the entire food chain. Animals starve and global famine looms. This leads to riots in city streets, the overthrow of governments and a breakdown in law and order.

Assuming human civilization can withstand the impact winter, an even greater challenge lies ahead as Earth begins to heat up. We could face rising sea levels from melting ice sheets, flooding of coasts and lowland areas, and increasingly turbulent weather. Exposure to UV light can lead to sunburn, skin cancer and damage to eyes and the **immune system**.

After impact

"The dust cloud would shield the Earth from ultraviolet light for an extended period ... After that, the ozone depletion would cause levels of ultraviolet radiation to at least double, about 600 days after impact."

Andrew Blaustein, Professor of Zoology at Oregon State University, USA

How would we adapt?

Life would certainly have to change, but it would be possible for the human race to survive an asteroid impact on this scale, providing people are willing to work together and make sacrifices. During the impact winter there would be severe shortages of food and other essentials. In places where government authority survives, a system of rationing would need to be imposed, placing strict limits on how much each person is allowed to purchase. Elsewhere, the situation could turn very ugly, with gangs fighting over what limited resources there are, and many people forced to beg for food.

The period of global warming would probably last much longer, perhaps even decades, and it may be accompanied by an increase in UV radiation due to damage to the ozone layer. For both these reasons, humans would have to stay indoors during daylight hours and adopt a more **nocturnal** lifestyle. Until temperatures return to normal and the ozone layer repairs itself, we would have to find ways of growing food on indoor farms.

What can we do?

Our planet is just one of millions of rocks whizzing at tremendous speeds through space. It's inevitable that our rock will, from time to time, collide with other rocks. So what can we do?

Watching the skies

Most importantly, we can keep a constant lookout for rocks heading towards us. The more warning we get of a collision, the more time we'll have to plan for it. We may even be able to launch a space mission to intercept the approaching rock (see page 47). The most dangerous rocks are those whose orbits bring them close to Earth, or near-Earth objects (NEOs). They include asteroids and comets. The type of NEO that poses the greatest threat are near-Earth asteroids (NEAs).

Since the 1990s, observatories around the world have been busy identifying NEAs. By July 2013, they had tracked 9,925 NEAs, 861 of which are 1 kilometre (0.6 mile) in diameter or larger. NEAs with orbits that could bring them close to Earth are called potentially hazardous asteroids (PHAs). According to NASA, there are currently 1,397 PHAs. The Minor Planet Center states that there are 1,409 PHAs.

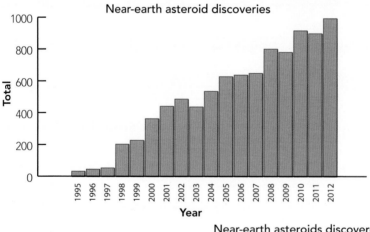

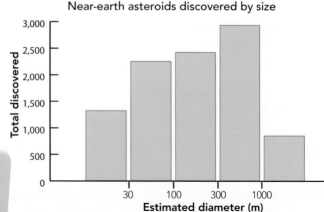

These charts show NEA discoveries over time and by size.

The Institute for Astronomy on Maui, Hawaii. One of the telescopes situated here is Pan-STARRS (Panoramic Survey Telescope and Rapid Response System), used to track objects such as meteors and asteroids that could come close to Earth.

Why wasn't the Chelyabinsk meteor spotted?

One of the most disturbing aspects of the Chelyabinsk meteor was that it came without warning. With so many telescopes scanning the heavens, why did no one see it coming? One reason was its small size. More than 99 per cent of the 9,925 NEAs so far spotted have been bigger than 100 metres (328 feet) in diameter – the Chelyabinsk meteor was less than a fifth of that.

The asteroid also arrived during the daytime, and astronomical observations are more easily done at night. Furthermore, it approached from the direction of the Sun, and the Sun's glare prevented ground-based telescopes from seeing it.

Missed opportunity

Scientists differ in their views about whether the Chelyabinsk meteor could have been detected before it struck:

"It was impossible to detect it, because it was flying from the Sun. But if it was flying at night, our MASTER telescope network could have traced it."

Sergei Lamzin, Deputy Director of the Sternberg Astronomical Institute at Moscow State University

"It would be very faint and difficult to detect, not impossible, but difficult."

Paul Chodas, research scientist at the Near Earth Object Program Office at the Jet Propulsion Laboratory, Pasadena, California

What have we learned?

For many scientists and politicians, the Chelyabinsk meteor was a wake-up call: it was time to take a closer look at smaller NEAs. "I think that what surprised most people was the scale of the damage from a relatively small object and the fact that we didn't have any warning," said Dr Hugh Lewis, Lecturer in Aerospace Engineering at the University of Southampton.

In June 2013, NASA announced its new ambition: to track any space rock big enough to cause damage, including those less than 10 metres (33 feet) wide. NASA admitted it didn't yet know how it would achieve this goal, but it invited individuals and private companies to come forward with suggestions.

Telescopes in space

One of the main problems is that NASA and other NEA-tracking organizations lack the resources to locate so many faint celestial bodies. What they need are bigger telescopes, in more locations. Especially

Space-based telescopes are likely to prove very useful in the hunt for the million or so smaller "city-busting" asteroids.

useful would be more telescopes in space. Earth-based telescopes suffer from a major disadvantage: sunlight masks their view of the heavens during the day, and at night the atmosphere distorts the light coming into their lenses (the same distortion that causes the stars to twinkle). By contrast: "A space-based asteroid hunter is … helpful because it can seek out space rocks at all hours of the day, as opposed to just at night," says Don Yeomans, manager of NASA's Near-Earth Object Program. The proposed space telescope Sentinel, which could launch in the next decade if successfully funded, would have the additional advantage of using **infrared** light, making it easier for astronomers to find objects that are too dark to be seen in visible light.

ATLAS

Even with the help of more space-based telescopes, a small NEA heading for Earth may still slip through the net. As a back-up, the University of Hawaii (with funding from NASA) is setting up a "final warning" programme called the Asteroid Terrestrial-impact Last Alert System (ATLAS). The idea is to provide short-term warning of approaching NEAs. ATLAS will employ eight small telescopes that will scan the sky twice a night, more quickly but in less depth than regular NEA-hunting observatories. This will enable it to provide a three-week warning for a 120-metre (390-foot) diameter asteroid and a one-week warning for a 45-metre (150-foot) one. By calculating the trajectory, ATLAS would be able to pinpoint the impact zone within a kilometre or two, hopefully giving any nearby towns or cities enough time to evacuate residents.

Must do better

Not all experts are impressed with NASA's record in asteroid hunting:

"NASA has not even come close to finding and tracking the 1 million smaller asteroids that might only just wipe out a city, or perhaps collapse the world economy if they hit in the wrong place."

Ed Lu, former astronaut and CEO of the B612 Foundation, an organization building Sentinel, an NEA-hunting space telescope

---

The threat from bigger NEAs

Ideally, we would like more notice of an approaching asteroid than one to three weeks. With the bigger NEAs – those with diameters greater than 1 kilometre (0.6 miles) – this is certainly possible. In fact, NASA estimates that some 95 per cent of these larger NEAs have been identified and tracked, and we can tell from their orbits if any are likely to collide with Earth. Currently, our biggest threat comes from Asteroid 1950 DA, which has a diameter of 1.1 kilometres (0.69 miles) and may possibly collide with Earth on 16 March 2880.

Intercepting the asteroid

So what do we do if a big asteroid is heading for Earth? According to experts, we could prevent the collision by intercepting the asteroid. "There are three ways to deflect a dangerous asteroid: the gentle pull, the swift kick and by nuking it," says Alan Fitzsimmons, an astronomer at Queens University, Belfast. The method chosen will depend on the asteroid's size, composition, orbit and how much warning we get.

In the future, we may be able to use a spacecraft to deflect an asteroid from its collision course with Earth by firing a laser beam at it.

With plenty of warning, the "gentle pull" might be the best method. This would involve sending a very heavy spacecraft to hover close to the asteroid. The tiny gravitational pull created by the spacecraft should be enough, over a period of years, to shift the asteroid off its collision course. The "swift kick" entails a collision: a heavy spacecraft is flown into the asteroid, changing its orbit. A second "kick" may be needed if this doesn't work. The last and most desperate method is to "nuke" the asteroid. A nuclear bomb detonated near the asteroid would hopefully evaporate its surface layers and push it in the opposite direction. However, there is a risk that the asteroid may shatter, but continue in the same orbit: one big impact on Earth could be replaced by multiple smaller ones.

AIDA

The European Space Agency (ESA) is currently considering a mission to test the "swift kick" method of asteroid deflection. The mission is called Asteroid Impact and Deflection Assessment (AIDA) and the idea is to send up two spacecraft – one to collide with the asteroid and the other to observe the results. The likely target is Didymos, a pair of asteroids in orbit around each other, and set for a close approach to Earth in 2022. Hitting the smaller of the two asteroids should, in theory, change its orbit around the larger one.

Practice makes perfect

"The first attempt to deflect an asteroid should not be when it counts for real, because there are no doubt many surprises in store as we learn how to manipulate asteroids."

Ed Lu, physicist and former
NASA astronaut

An international issue

Any impending collision would, of course, be a concern for the entire world – so decisions on how to deal with such a crisis need to involve every country. Plans are already in place to create a Space Mission Planning Advisory Group (SMPAG), made up of scientists from NASA, ESA and the world's other space agencies.

SMPAG (pronounced *same-page*) will meet annually to discuss new ideas for deflecting or destroying dangerous asteroids. If an asteroid is discovered heading for Earth, SMPAG will immediately meet to decide how best to intercept it. They will advise on how to build the intercepting spacecraft, using experts from around the world.

Emergency response

In case the mission to intercept the asteroid fails, governments will need to plan for the ensuing disaster when the asteroid hits. By plotting the asteroid's trajectory, scientists should be able to calculate the impact zone some days before, hopefully allowing enough time to evacuate any nearby towns and cities, or coastal settlements bordering the ocean.

Government agencies, such as the Federal Emergency Management Agency (FEMA) in the United States, will need to act fast. They will have to use all forms of media to send out warnings and issue advice and instructions to the public. They should coordinate with local authorities, businesses and **NGOs** so that everyone is ready to deal, as best they can, with the coming disaster. They will need to provide for search and rescue staff and equipment, evacuee transportation, emergency accommodation, food and medicine, and public security.

Catching an asteroid

In June 2013, NASA proposed an ambitious plan to capture an asteroid. It has selected three small asteroids, each about 10 metres (30 feet) wide. They plan to use an unmanned solar-powered spacecraft to drag one of the asteroids into orbit around the Moon. A manned mission could then be sent to it, which will hopefully help develop knowledge and skills that we can use to avoid future impacts.

Some countries will be better equipped than others at dealing with the crisis. But wherever the asteroid hits, the world should act together to deal with the consequences, and less-affected countries should offer as much aid as required to the stricken regions. After all, it could just as easily have landed on them.

Being prepared

The Chelyabinsk meteor served as a valuable reminder to us all of the ever-present threat from our skies. These events are thankfully rare, but we need to be ready for them. Just as governments in earthquake-prone or flood-prone areas have plans in place for dealing with these types of emergencies, so governments around the world should be prepared to deal with an impact event. Of course, the difference between asteroids and other types of natural disaster is that an asteroid can strike anywhere!

An emergency management team carry out a training exercise. We must hope that there won't be a major asteroid impact in the foreseeable future, but if there is one, we need to be ready to deal with it.

Timeline

30 June 1908	The Tunguska event: a comet or asteroid explodes over a remote part of Siberia
26 November 1919	A meteor explodes above southern Michigan and northern Indiana, USA, breaking windows and knocking out communications and electrical power in several cities
28 April 1927	A meteorite injures a little girl in Aba, Japan – the first known meteorite injury
1947	The Minor Planet Center begins cataloguing the orbits of near-Earth asteroids and comets
30 November 1954	A meteorite injures Ann Hodges in Sylacauga, Alabama, USA
7 April 1959	A meteor strikes east of Příbram, Czech Republic: the first tracking of a meteor by several cameras, enabling scientists to plot its orbit and discover where it landed
10 August 1972	A meteor fireball is sighted during daylight above the western United States and Canada
8 March 1976	A meteor explodes over the outskirts of Jilin City, northern China, showering the local area with chondrites (chunks of meteorite). One turned out to be the largest chondrite ever found.
1996	The Spaceguard System is established – a global network of observatories responsible for identifying and tracking near-Earth objects
6 October 2008	For the first time, astronomers correctly predict an asteroid impact: 2008 TC3, which lands in Sudan on 7 October
15 February 2013	09.20.20 An asteroid enters Earth's atmosphere over the Kazakhstan/Russia border
15 February 2013	09.20.33 The asteroid (now a superbolide meteor) reaches its peak brightness and explodes

15 February 2013	09.22.40 The explosion's shockwave reaches Chelyabinsk
15 February 2013	10.05 (approx) (23.05 on 14 February, EST) News breaks in Washington, DC, USA, of an explosion in Chelyabinsk
16 February 2013	The first meteorite fragments go on sale on Russian internet auction sites
16–17 February 2013	Meteor-mania goes global as dashcam videos of the meteor are uploaded onto YouTube and viewed millions of times
19 February 2013	Affected schools and hospitals reopen
26 February 2013	It is announced that Colombian astronomers have plotted the orbit of the Chelyabinsk meteor
5 March 2013	The emergency situation is declared over
14 March 2013	All but four people injured in the Chelyabinsk meteor strike have left hospital
19 March 2013	Russian scientists announce weight and age of Chelyabinsk meteorite
21 March 2013	Russian scientists discover a crater beneath Lake Chebarkul caused by a large meteorite fragment
June 2013	NASA invites experts to present ideas on capturing an asteroid

Glossary

accretion gradual build-up of additional layers

air burst explosion in the air

bolide large meteor that explodes in the atmosphere

carbon dioxide gas that is given off when fossil fuels such as coal, oil and natural gas are burned. It is called a greenhouse gas because it traps heat from the Sun in Earth's atmosphere and adds to the greenhouse effect.

celestial body natural objects visible in the sky

chondrite stony meteorite that contains small particles of iron and nickel

comet object with a core of ice and dust that, when near the Sun, forms a long tail of gas and dust particles

concussion temporary unconsciousness caused by a blow to the head

dashcam camera fitted to the dashboard of a car and used to record traffic incidents

Eastern Standard Time Five hours behind the current time in the UK. The eastern US, Canada and parts of eastern South America fall into this time zone.

gradient angle of slope

gravitational influence force of attraction between masses, such as a planet and its moons

greenhouse effect the trapping of the Sun's warmth by gases in Earth's atmosphere

ground-penetrating radar the use of radar pulses to create an image of something below the ground's surface

Hertz unit of frequency, used for measuring sound waves

Hiroshima Japanese city that was the target of the world's first atomic bomb, dropped by US Army Air Forces on 6 August 1945, near the end of World War II

immune system organs and processes of the body that provide resistance to infection

impact winter prolonged period of cold weather caused by the impact of a large asteroid

infrared form of electromagnetic radiation just beyond the red end of the visible light spectrum

infrastructure buildings, roads, power supplies and other basic structures and facilities needed for the operation of a society or business

kiloton unit of explosive power equivalent to 1,000 tonnes of an explosive material called TNT

looting stealing from a damaged or empty property

media term used to describe radio, television, newspapers, magazines and the internet

megaton unit of explosive power equivalent to one million tonnes of TNT (an explosive material)

meteor streak of light in the sky caused by a meteoroid entering the atmosphere

meteorite debris of a meteoroid that survives its passage through the atmosphere and hits Earth's surface

meteoroid small object of up to 1 metre (3.3 feet) in diameter that moves through the solar system

National Aeronautics and Space Administration (NASA) agency of the United States government responsible for the nation's civilian space programme and for aeronautics and aerospace research

nerve agent one of a class of phosphorus-containing chemicals that are lethal to humans

nocturnal of the night

non-government organization (NGO) non-profit organization that is not part of a national government and pursues a social or political goal. Examples include the United Nations, Red Cross and Greenpeace.

nuclear test test carried out to determine the effectiveness of a nuclear weapon

oblast administrative division in Russia and other countries of the former Soviet Union, often translated as "area", "zone", "province" or "region"

observatory building that houses an astronomical telescope

ozone layer layer in Earth's atmosphere, around 15–35 kilometres (9–22 miles) from the surface, containing a high concentration of the gas ozone

photosynthesis process by which plants use sunlight to create energy from carbon dioxide and water

plastic surgery surgery involving the reconstruction or repair of parts of the body, either to treat injury or for cosmetic reasons

plutonium radioactive chemical element used as a fuel in nuclear reactors and as an explosive in nuclear weapons

post-traumatic stress disorder condition of mental and emotional stress resulting from injury or severe psychological shock

radiation energy and particles given out by something. Nuclear radiation is dangerous to living organisms and so nuclear reactors are heavily shielded.

radioactive waste waste material containing harmful radiation that is a by-product of nuclear power generation

shockwave wave formed by the sudden compression (e.g. by an earthquake or explosion) of the substance through which the wave travels

sonic boom loud, explosive noise caused by the shockwave of an object travelling faster than the speed of sound

sublime change from solid to gas state without a liquid phase in between

superbolide extremely bright and large meteor that explodes in the atmosphere

telecommunication satellites artificial bodies placed in orbit around Earth for the purpose of communication

TNT (trinitrotoluene) highly explosive material

trajectory path followed by a moving object

tsunami huge wave caused by an earthquake, undersea landslide, asteroid impact or other disturbance

ultraviolet (UV) form of electromagnetic radiation just beyond the violet end of the visible light spectrum. Ultraviolet radiation is part of sunlight, although the ozone layer prevents much of it from reaching the Earth's surface.

vaporize convert into vapour

weapons-grade material that is suitable for making nuclear weapons

Find out more

Non-fiction books

An Asteroid Strike (A World After), Alex Woolf (Raintree, 2013)

Asteroids and the Asteroid Belt (Explore Outer Space), Ruth Owen (Windmill Books, 2012)

Comets, Asteroids and Meteors (Astronaut Travel Guides), Stuart Atkinson (Raintree, 2012)

Exploring Dangers in Space: Asteroids, Space Junk, and More (Searchlight Books: What's Amazing about Space), Buffy Silverman (Lerner Classroom, 2011)

Fiction books

Asteroid, Mark Cooke (Nightingale Books, 2004)

Asteroid (Shades), Malcolm Rose (Evans Brothers, 2009)

Asteroid Strike (Future Tense), Michael Johnstone (Franklin Watts, 2000)

Films

Armageddon (1998, 12 certificate)
This is a science-fiction drama about a space mission sent by NASA to stop a "Texas-sized" asteroid on a collision course with Earth.

Cosmic Collisions: Our Explosive Universe (2009)
This documentary discusses near-Earth objects and the threat they pose.

Deep Impact (1998, 12 certificate)
This science-fiction drama describes the attempts to prepare for and destroy an 11-kilometre (7-mile) wide comet headed for Earth.

Horizon: The Truth About Meteors (2013)
Produced in the wake of the Chelyabinsk meteor strike, this documentary explores what meteorites and asteroids are, where they come from and the danger they pose.

NOVA: Meteor Strike (2013)
This is a documentary about the Chelyabinsk meteor strike.

Websites

www.killerasteroids.org
On this website you can play a physics-based asteroid game, learn about how amateur astronomers are contributing to asteroid research, or carry out a simulated asteroid strike on any location in the world.

www.nasa.gov/centers/ames/about/overview.html
The NASA Ames Research Center looks at asteroid and comet impact hazards.

www.nasa.gov/mission_pages/WISE/news/wise20120516.html
This section of the official NASA website gives up-to-date news about the search for near-Earth objects.

neo.jpl.nasa.gov/news/fireball_130301.html
This section of the NASA website gives information about the Chelyabinsk meteor.

www.purdue.edu/impactearth
This site is another asteroid impact calculator in which you enter information about an imaginary strike and it tells you the destructive effects.

www.spaceguarduk.com
The Spaceguard Centre UK is the British branch of an international effort to detect near-Earth objects.

More topics to research

1. Research and write your own "disaster dossier" on a meteor strike not mentioned in this book. Examples could include the fireball witnessed above New York City, USA, on 15 November 1859, the meteorite shower near Helsinki, Finland, on 12 March 1899, or the so-called "Brazilian Tunguska event" near the Curuçá River Area, Amazonas, Brazil, of 13 August 1930.

2. Imagine you are the head of an emergency management agency in a city and you've just been informed that a 20-metre (60-foot) wide asteroid is heading towards your region, due to strike in around 20 hours. What actions could you take now to minimize loss of life and long-term damage to your city?

3. Take a look at the down2EARTH Impact Calculator at education.down2earth.eu/impact_calculator.
Select values to describe an asteroid strike of your choice, then click "submit" to discover the consequences. Try entering different values and see what difference it makes. What factors cause the most damage as you increase them: asteroid diameter, trajectory angle, object velocity or projectile density?

Index